WITHDRAWN

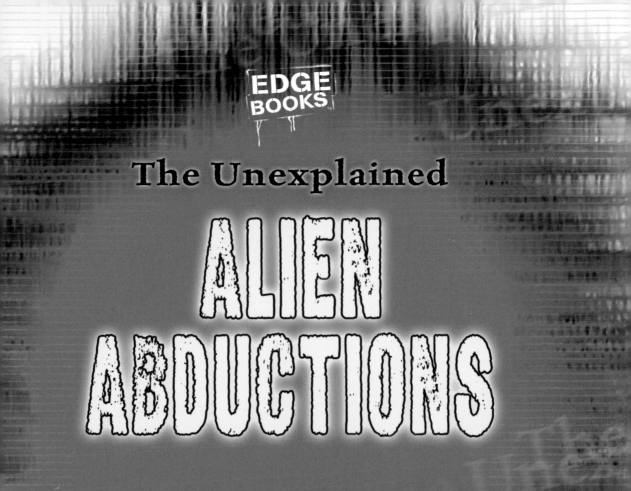

EDGE BOOKS

The Unexplained

ALIEN ABDUCTIONS

by **Michael Martin**
Consultant:
Jerome Clark, Co-editor
International UFO Reporter
J. Allen Hynek Center for UFO Studies
Chicago, Illinois

Capstone
press

Mankato, Minnesota

Edge Books are published by Capstone Press,
151 Good Counsel Drive, P.O. Box 669, Mankato, Minnesota 56002.
www.capstonepress.com

Library of Congress Cataloging-in-Publication Data
Martin, Michael, 1948–
    Alien abductions / by Michael Martin.
    p. cm.—(Edge books. The unexplained)
    Includes bibliographical references and index.
    ISBN-13: 978-0-7368-4380-5 (hardcover)
    ISBN-10: 0-7368-4380-9 (hardcover)
    1. Alien abduction—Juvenile literature. I. Title. II. Series.
BF2050.M355 2006
001.942—dc22   2005018485

Summary: Describes alien abduction experiences and the search for answers.

Editorial Credits
Katy Kudela, editor; Juliette Peters, set designer; Kate Opseth and Thomas Emery,
    book designers; Kelly Garvin, photo researcher/photo editor

Photo Credits
Corbis/Bettmann, 11
Fortean Picture Library, 15, 17, 24; Amilton Vieira, 25; Andrew C. Stewart,
    9, 23, 29; Dezso Sternoczky/SUFOI, cover; Dr. Susan Blackmore, 27;
    Paul Villa, 8
Mary Evans Picture Library, 5, 12, 19, 21; Michael Buhler, 7, 13, 26

TABLE OF CONTENTS

FEATURES

Chapter 1

KIDNAPPED BY ALIENS?

Early one morning in August 1993, Kelly and Andrew Cahill were driving home. Suddenly, they saw a large flying object. It hovered above the road not far from the town of Belgrave, Australia. The round object had windows. Lights shone brightly around the bottom. Kelly thought she saw figures moving inside. The flying object quickly streaked away.

A little farther down the road, a bright light blinded Kelly and Andrew. The next instant, the sky was empty.

Learn about:
• Cahill abduction
• Lost memories
• Meeting aliens

The flying objects that many people claim to have seen look like a ring of light, such as this object photographed in New Zealand.

As they continued their drive home, Kelly and Andrew began to argue. They both felt something odd had happened to them. But they had little memory of the event. When the Cahills arrived home, they noticed the trip had taken 90 minutes longer than usual.

A few weeks later, Kelly was rushed to the hospital. She had a bad infection. The doctors told her one of two things must have happened. Either she was pregnant or she must have just had surgery. Neither was true.

Scary Memories

Kelly began having nightmares. In her dreams, she was lying on a table unable to move. A dark figure stood over her. A few months later, Kelly's nightmares gave way to memories. She remembered a huge spacecraft landing beside the road. Tall beings surrounded the cars on the road. "We mean you no harm," they said. Then they took Kelly and two other women into the spacecraft.

▲ In her nightmares, Kelly Cahill recalled meeting strange beings from outer space.

Kelly wasn't sure if her memories were real. She contacted researchers who study unidentified flying objects (UFOs). They ran newspaper ads to see if other people had seen anything strange. Two women came forward. Their reports matched Kelly's story. They even had physical symptoms like Kelly's.

▲ **People claim they have seen UFOs during the day and at night.**

Abduction Stories

Kelly Cahill's story is not unique. Thousands of people around the world have reported alien abductions. The staggering number of reports has researchers searching for answers. Can so many people be wrong? Are aliens really visiting earth?

Many people believe in alien abductions. They say that the stories can't be ignored. But others want more proof. Researchers today are still trying to solve the mystery of alien abductions.

▼ Artists often draw aliens as scary creatures.

Chapter 2

Early Alien Abductions

The first reports of alien abductions started in the 1950s. Some people claimed they rode aboard spacecrafts with friendly aliens. Few people believed these stories.

During the 1960s, people began reporting new alien visits. These aliens weren't as friendly. People reported being kidnapped by aliens.

One of the first frightening encounters with aliens was reported by Betty and Barney Hill. On September 19, 1961, the Hills were driving at night on a lonely stretch of highway in New Hampshire. An object that looked like a bright star followed their car. They stopped to look at the object with binoculars. It looked like a spacecraft.

Learn about:
- Early alien encounters
- Hypnosis
- Childhood memories

Betty and Barney Hill claimed aliens kidnapped them. They had detailed memories of a spacecraft and aliens.

The frightened couple quickly drove away. On their drive home, Betty and Barney heard strange beeps. When they arrived home, they were tired and puzzled. Their trip had taken much longer than it should have.

Both the Hills believe they saw a spacecraft hovering in the sky.

Strange Stories

Two years later, Barney became sick with stomach problems. A doctor thought stress might be causing Barney's pain. The doctor put Barney in a hypnotic trance to help him remember what was worrying him. Barney remembered being taken aboard a spacecraft.

Betty was also hypnotized. She told a similar story. She remembered creatures with blue-gray skin and eyes that wrapped around their heads.

Man Goes Missing

In 1975, some Arizona loggers spotted a UFO in the sky. One of the men, 22-year-old Travis Walton, decided to take a closer look. As his friends watched, Walton walked toward the UFO. Suddenly, a beam of light knocked him down. Thinking he was dead, the friends got scared and ran away. Later, their search for Walton's body turned up nothing.

After five days, Walton suddenly reappeared. He had very strange memories to share with his family and friends. After being struck by the beam of light, Walton remembered waking up in what looked like a hospital room. He turned to see aliens standing over him. Frightened, he fought his way out of the room. He then met a tall human man who directed him to another room. There, he met other humans who gently guided him to a table. The next thing Walton remembered was waking up on the side of a highway.

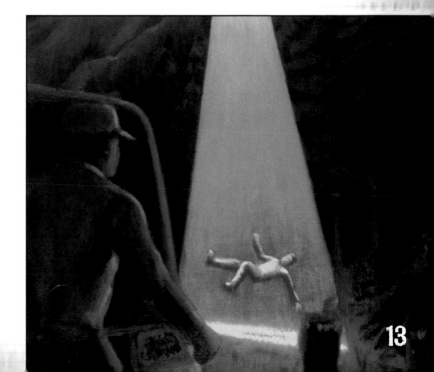

Buried Memories

Memories of alien abductions are seldom clear. Some people go years before they can recall what happened.

Whitley Strieber, a U.S. author, has had strange memories since he was a young boy. He remembered beings with dark eyes and pointed chins giving him a medical examination.

As an adult, Strieber wanted to find explanations for these odd memories. After being hypnotized, Strieber remembered more details. He came to believe aliens abducted him.

In 1987, Strieber began to write books about his alien abduction experiences. His books encouraged others to talk. Strieber received thousands of letters from people who thought they might have been abducted too.

EDGE FACT

Many abductees report seeing the same type of alien. These creatures have gray skin, large heads, and large eyes. Their mouths, noses, and ears are smaller than those of humans.

▲ People who have memories of an alien abduction sometimes try to draw pictures of what they saw. An abductee from the United States drew this picture.

Chapter 3

STUDYING STORIES

For the past 50 years, researchers have been studying alien abductions. Budd Hopkins is one of the best-known researchers. He has met with hundreds of people who believe they have been kidnapped by aliens.

Hopkins uses hypnosis to help people remember their experiences. While in a sleeplike trance, these people often report gaps in their memory. Many people also remember strange dreams and events they can't explain. Some even admit they avoid certain places because they think something awful happened to them there.

Learn about:
• Budd Hopkins
• Evidence
• False memories

Dreams may shed light on hidden memories. The creator of this painting drew scenes from his frequent dreams about aliens.

Similar Stories

Many stories that Hopkins listened to had the same details. People reported being taken against their will. They remember going aboard an alien spacecraft. Inside the spacecraft, aliens studied human bodies.

David Jacobs is an associate professor of history at Philadelphia's Temple University. After meeting Hopkins, he became curious about alien abductions. He also learned how to use hypnosis.

Jacobs has hypnotized hundreds of people claiming to be abductees. Their stories were similar to the stories Hopkins had heard. Abductees often said they were drawn toward a powerful light. Many reported meeting alien beings that examined them. Few people remember details about the exams. There is almost always a period of time they can't remember.

▲ Images of being inside an alien spacecraft show up in some abductees' dreams.

Hopkins' research has changed the minds of some skeptics. John Mack, who died in 2004, was a psychiatrist and a professor at Harvard University. He thought people made up stories to tell Hopkins. But Mack spoke with abductees himself. He found that people honestly believe that aliens abducted them.

Problems with Hypnosis

Not everyone believes in hypnotic research. Some researchers don't think hypnosis can be trusted. Hypnosis can produce false memories. Psychologist William Cone warns that the wrong kind of questions can encourage a hypnotized person to tell fake stories.

Physical Evidence

Abductees often find mysterious scars or cuts on their bodies. Some people believe these marks are proof that aliens kidnapped them.

Many abductees report small objects placed in their noses by alien examiners. One abductee removed a small, wire-like fiber from her nose. She turned it over to researcher John Mack. He had other scientists study the object. Experts claimed the fiber was not something found in nature. They thought the fiber was a manufactured item. But they could not tell who made it.

▼ **A grid-pattern burn appeared on this man. He said he got the burn after looking at a UFO that had landed on the ground.**

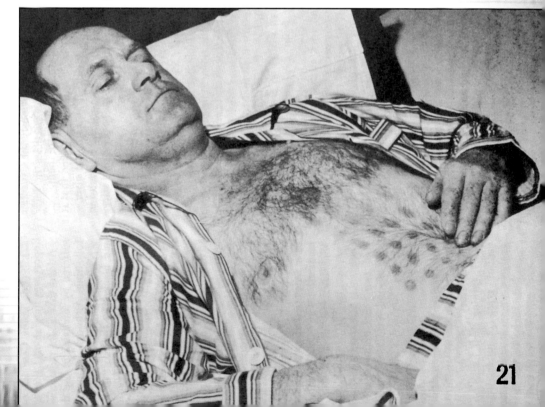

Chapter 4

LOOKING FOR ANSWERS

Solving the mystery of alien abductions is difficult. Reports of abductions come in from all over the world. Although their reports are similar, people who report being abducted have little in common. People who have claimed to be abducted work in different kinds of jobs. They range in age from young to old.

The time and place of reported alien abductions is not always the same. People say they have seen aliens in the early morning and late at night. Some abductees remember being kidnapped at home. Others say they met aliens while driving their cars or walking outside.

Learn about:
- What skeptics believe
- People's fears
- Helpful aliens

According to many reports, alien spacecrafts seem to appear out of nowhere.

Hollywood Ideas

Some people don't believe in alien abductions. They say TV shows, movies, books, and magazines give people ideas about aliens. Some skeptics believe these ideas are stored in the memory and then appear in dreams. People who have these dreams may then report a false abduction.

Physical Proof Versus Stories

Scientists who are skeptics want to find stronger proof. They think many people who report abductions are dishonest or simply mistaken. These scientists are looking for physical proof to show that aliens exist. They want to find a piece of metal from a UFO or a photograph of a real alien.

▼ Science fiction magazines may be one source of people's strange dreams.

In March 1988, John Salter Jr. and his son said they were abducted by aliens. After returning to earth, Salter noticed his hair and nails grew faster and a scar on his forehead faded.

↑ Many UFO photos are unclear. Bright lights may have caused a UFO-shaped object to appear In this photo taken in Brazil.

Researchers like Hopkins and Jacobs look for patterns in the stories of abductees. They say most abductees seem sincere. When people recall their abductions, they seem truly scared. But the stories raise questions. Why are aliens visiting? Do the aliens have plans for humans?

▲ **Most abductees tell stories that have the same details. They often remember aliens taking them aboard a spacecraft.**

Hopkins doesn't know for sure what aliens are doing. But he doesn't trust them. He believes aliens can make abductees forget what happened to them. He also thinks aliens can put false memories into people's minds.

Jacobs doesn't trust aliens either. Many abductees have told Jacobs they have seen babies on alien spacecrafts. Jacobs believes aliens are trying to create a new nation of beings that are part alien and part human.

▼ Some people believe aliens have the power to change abductees' memories.

A Positive Outlook

Mack had a more positive view of aliens. He met abductees who said aliens cured them of diseases. Other abductees gave Mack a sense that aliens are trying to warn humans. Abductees say aliens have shown them pictures of what earth will look like if humans don't care for it better. The aliens' warnings have been so strong that some abductees are working to improve the planet.

Mack wondered if contact with aliens would help humans. Meanwhile, he said that reported alien abductions are changing the beliefs of people around the world. More and more people are having a difficult time ignoring the idea of other beings living in the universe.

Common Goal

No matter what their beliefs are, the goal of all researchers is to figure out what is happening. Researchers want to know whether the stories of thousands of abductees are true. If the stories are true, what do they mean for humans?

⬆ The idea of aliens traveling to earth is in many fiction stories. But millions of people believe aliens really do visit earth.

GLOSSARY

abduction (ab-DUKT-shuhn)—a kidnapping; a person who is kidnapped is an abductee.

alien (AY-lee-uhn)—a creature from another planet

examination (eg-zam-uh-NAY-shuhn)—a careful medical check of a person's body

hypnotize (HIP-nuh-tize)—to put another person into a sleeplike state; people sometimes recall memories better when hypnotized.

skeptic (SKEP-tic)—a person who questions things that other people believe in

symptom (SIMP-tuhm)—a sign of an illness or a disease

trance (TRANSS)—a sleeplike condition in which a person is conscious but not completely aware of what is happening around them

READ MORE

Herbst, Judith. *Aliens.* Unexplained. Minneapolis: Lerner, 2005.

Sievert, Terri. *UFOs.* Edge Books: The Unexplained. Mankato, Minn.: Capstone Press, 2005.

Silverstein, Janna. *Close Encounters with Aliens.* Unsolved Mysteries. New York: Rosen Central, 2002.

INTERNET SITES

FactHound offers a safe, fun way to find Internet sites related to this book. All of the sites on FactHound have been researched by our staff.

Here's how:
1. Visit *www.facthound.com*
2. Type in this special code **0736843809** for age-appropriate sites. Or enter a search word related to this book for a more general search.
3. Click on the **Fetch It** button.

FactHound will fetch the best sites for you!

INDEX

WITHDRAWN